NORWICH

Edited by Claire Tupholme

First published in Great Britain in 2003 by
YOUNG WRITERS
Remus House,
Coltsfoot Drive,
Peterborough, PE2 9JX
Telephone (01733) 890066

SB ISBN 1 84460 239 7

FOREWORD

Young Writers was established in 1991 as a foundation for promoting the reading and writing of poetry amongst children and young adults. Today it continues this quest and proceeds to nurture and guide the writing talents of today's youth.

From this year's competition Young Writers is proud to present a showcase of the best poetic talent from across the UK. Each hand-picked poem has been carefully chosen from over 66,000 'Hullabaloo!' entries to be published in this, our eleventh primary school series.

This year in particular we have been wholeheartedly impressed with the quality of entries received. The thought, effort, imagination and hard work put into each poem impressed us all and once again the task of editing was a difficult but enjoyable experience.

We hope you are as pleased as we are with the final selection and that you and your family will continue to be entertained with *Hullabaloo! Norwich* for many years to come.

CONTENTS

The Poems

I Am A Dog

I am a dog, I'm black and white,
Some people love, some I give a fright.

I'm let out in the garden cos I need a wee,
I wee up a fence and I wee up a tree.

A cat's near my back door, it's good enough to catch,
It jumped on my gate and knocked open the latch.

I ran without thinking, I flew through the gate,
Hoping the cat would soon meet its fate.

I ran down the alley and never stopped running,
The plans in my head were rather cunning.

The car ran across the small, quiet road,
But just as I crossed I saw a big load!

A van was coming, I thought I would die,
I'd go up on the bonnet, in mid-air I'd fly.

The impact was painful, the impact was strong,
I knew from the start that the cat chase was wrong.

I woke up in a building, a place called the vet's,
A place where they treated sick, injured pets.

My leg really hurt, I was in pain,
I know I will never chase a cat again.

Arran Starling (10)

LONG LIVE THE LAST

In blustery skies the dragons fought.
The Holy dragon was already weakened,
His right shoulder impaled on a horn.
The blame-worthy dragon,
A corrupt,
Beastly thing,
Took the Holy in his jaws,
Then,
Keeping its grip,
Began pelting sweltering fireballs
Through the dying Holy's entrails.
With a severely damaged left wing,
The Holy fell,
Spinning to the ground,
Dead.
Long live the last.

Joey Kuna (10)
Colman Middle School

HONEYCOMBS AND BLACKBIRDS

The sky, an alluring blue with frail white clouds,
Pink and white blossom gliding through the air
like a swan without a care in the world.
The sun, a facet of glistening crimson over a commencing sunset.
A forest almost silent but for a mysterious,
eerie mist circling the swaying trees.
Only a few miniscule movements throughout the land
indicates anything living.
When evening comes, the wistful stars gaze upon
a harmonic landscape.
The night's noises resound in the leaves and a lone bee
makes a buzzing sound, echoing across a vast valley.
As summer reaches the borders of a world of peace,
an aura of liveliness starts to dance in the air.

Ryan Roffey (11)
Colman Middle School

The Shadow

My dream horse galloping across the field,
Mane tossing and rippling in the wind.
Muscles stretching and tightening,
Flying into the moonlight.
Neck arched; tail swishing,
A thundering of hooves.
Coat shining and gleaming,
As if an angel is flying through the air.
Beauty fills the cold crisp night.
As this shadow floats past.
Could this be real?

Kathryn Harvey (11)
Colman Middle School

WHY?

Why does there have to be global warming,
animals dying with nowhere to live
and kids who can't go out?
    Why?
Why does there have to be bombs
and terrorists who destroy things?
Thousands of people die because of bombs,
    Why?
Why are there people dying in South Africa
with no water?
Why don't we do something for all these topics
because even the smallest things count?
    Why?

Kris Coidan (11)
Colman Middle School

Why? Why?

Why, why do we pretend to beg?
Why, why do we like destroying things?
Why, why do we go to war?
Why, why do we kill endangered animals?
Why, why do we burn fossil fuels?
Why, why we do use guns to get our own way?
Why, why do we drink ourselves stupid?
Why, why do we take drugs?

Only mad people,
Sick people,
Dumb people,
Weird people,
Jealous people
And poor people like these things.

So don't like them!

Ian Harrison (10)
Colman Middle School

Queen Bee

One breezy midday a jet-black and golden queen bee
Was gently floating about in the air
Her teeny tiny flying carriage calmly springing around
Suddenly she exclaimed, 'Stop!' to her driving workers
But it was too late, they had fallen down a human's throat
They saw talking dolphins in a water world
Candyfloss streets with chocolate lamp posts
And the best buzzy bee theme park ever
Soon the queen bee found a honey trail
She wandered off eating away at the surroundings
She became fatter and fatter
Eventually as plump as a plum!

Siberiana Longordo (10)
Colman Middle School

Hustling Streets

The lamp posts are rattling
The trees are twinkly like stars
Chocolates are falling off the trees
Strawberries are squinting out the lamp posts
Dragons blowing fire
Goblins chasing each other round the streets.

Joshua Pinder (11)
Colman Middle School

My Fantasy Land

If I picked my own world it would be like a Hawaiian place
The sky would be a baby pink with lovely purple clouds
It would have a beautiful pond with magical fish
It would be the best place to chill out
Dolphins would leap in the wonderful fresh air
There would be a hotel suite with a view of Hollywood
A huge swimming pool with palm trees for shade
And every night to finish off the day, we would have a huge swimming party
This would be my dream world.

Amy Batch (11)
Colman Middle School

SHIMMER

The gentle, long cod with piercing blue eyes
Her frantic twitchiness in her sleep
Her rough pink tongue against your skin
Her tiger-like ways, the way she stalks her prey
And her long white dagger teeth
Her fun, clever ways inspired other cats
As she glides expertly through the night
Enjoying company from other felines
And then gently and quietly sleeping
On a soft, black mat.

Rebecca Self (10)
Colman Middle School

Street Life

The hustling and bustling down the busy streets
Drain covers creak and money falls
The hum of voices while street lamps flicker
A dog pulls on its lead when it sees a passing cat
The delightful smell of fresh bread wafts out of the bakery
The occasional bag drops and the contents scatter across the pavement
A boy stands staring at life passing by
Will it ever stop?

Peter Slorach (10)
Colman Middle School

Fantasy

Yummy Land is a place for everyone - girls, boys, young and old
It's set far, far away from everything but all you have to do is
Wish, wish and wish
The fluffy pink clouds are made out of soft, tasty candyfloss
Gently floating in the light blue sky
Just like the oceans drifting to the shore
The rainbow's colours twinkle and the sherbet strips sprinkle
The wacky funfair shimmers with lights
The candy swings and the chocolate rides - yummy for my tummy
The candy gates with curls and swirls stand as still as a statue
With red and white stripes glazed with sugar
Now the magnificent caramel sun slowly falls down into the seabed
Going, going, going, gone.

Chelsea Marley (10)
Colman Middle School

Clouds

I see the clouds which look like snow
I wish I could hold them
I see the clouds which look like fur
I wish I could stroke them
I se the clouds which move around
I wish I could fly them
And maybe one day
I will.

Megan Strike (11)
Colman Middle School

Me

This poem is about me
What can I say?
I'm just so happy
You would think I'd won the lottery every day

My family think I'm mad
But I just blame it on my dad
They say I'm worse after school
I say it's up to me
Cos I rule!

Chloe Buxton (11)
Colman Middle School

Sunset

As I stare into the sky,
The sun is setting elegantly.
A magnificent ball of fire in the beautiful world of dreams
Gleaming with exquisite colours,
Like a soft quilt of pinks and reds.
It fascinates me to stand and look at the amazing view.
Suddenly as the night approaches,
A new land of sleep awaits
As I stare into the darkness.

Shereen Boudjelal (11)
Colman Middle School

Colours

The trees are brown
The bins are red
The sky is blue
And overlooks your head
But have you ever thought about in another land?

The trees are pink
The bins are purple
The sky is green
So as people have seen
But what about the things outside of space?

The trees aren't there
Neither are any bins
The sky is black
Not at all like Blu- tac.
But not in the normal world.

Katrina Turner (10)
Colman Middle School

The Black Panther

Noble and proud as a lion, king of the jungle
As fast and sure-footed as a rabbit chased by a hound
Playful as a kitten who caught its first mouse
Sly and cunning as a puma creeping
As sleek and agile as an arrow gliding through the air
Alert but content sitting on a branch
A deep rumbling purr of relaxation sounds through silence
He yawns, sharp teeth gleaming in the sun
Sleep drawing near as he lies down
His almond-amber eyes blink
Open . . close . . . open
Close.

Carey Lang (10)
Colman Middle School

SPACE

As I float through space with zero gravity
I see Venus with its sandy hills
I then see Saturn with its icy, rocky ring
And then as I'm floating through space I see an alien on Mars
I see home . . . Earth!
Just then I see the blazing hot sun
I see a shower of meteorites coming from the plant Pluto
And Mercury as plain and brown as ever
And last but not least, Jupiter with its faint ring
And all of the dazzling stars.

Duncan Osborne (10)
Colman Middle School

Nothing

I've got nothing in my mind
About anything at all,
My head is shared with blackness,
My head is blank like walls.

I tell you that there is nothing
I can think of at all,
I've tried really hard to
But my mind can't take it in.

I've just realised
That all I have to do
Is write a poem about nothing
And there it is . . . for you.

Chloe Thomson (9)
Falcon Middle School

Nothing

I can't describe what's going on,
There's a funny sort of feeling,
I'm lost in my mind.

I don't know what to think,
It's so blank,
Empty darkness is all around me.

It's so strange, so indescribable,
I haven't been here before,
There's nothing here to touch.

This is just so strange,
It's so large and big,
It's like I'm in a rainforest,
But there's no bugs, trees or landscape
And I'm lost.

Jack Sexton (10)
Falcon Middle School

NOTHING

I can only think of nothing,
I have a blank mind,
Nothing is my hobby,
There isn't anything inside.
Nothing is my speciality,
I am really bored of nothing,
There's always something in nothing,
I can only think of nothing . . .

Marcus Wohlgemuth (9)
Falcon Middle School

Nothing

I just can't put my finger on it,
This place is indescribable.
As I fall down, it's just pitch-black,
Nothing to see or hear or do.

As I wander in this place,
I think of merely nothing,
My mind so blank,
My head so empty.

This place looks familiar,
No, it's gone, I can't see it.
It's there, it's finished,
I'm out of this world and in my own.

Jordan Antonietti (10)
Falcon Middle School

Nothing

I'm in a room of darkness,
There's nothing around,
I get an idea of what I could do,
But soon I begin to think that's idiotic too.

I look out of the window,
I see a passer-by.
I start looking round the room,
Suddenly I see some crystals
Glimmering in the window.
Wait, I've written a poem.

Michael Jones (10)
Falcon Middle School

NOTHING

My life is full of nothing,
There's nothing on the wall,
Nothing where I'm walking,
Nothing anywhere!

There's nothing laid across the floor,
There's nothing in my school,
Nothing on the football score,
Nothing anywhere!

My mind is full of nothing,
There's nothing on my page,
There isn't any lead in my pencil,
Still nothing anywhere!

Nothing in the forest,
Except trees and bugs,
When you think about it,
There must be something, somewhere!

I'm on an African safari,
I haven't seen anything yet,
But then animals from all directions come,
There's lots of things in Africa.

I get home after my long journey,
I've seen lots of things on my way,
I know that there is not just nothing,
I know that there is everything!

So finally, I see that there is something,
I just can't believe there's everything.
I've been stupid to think that there's nothing,
Because there's everything in the world.

George Frost (10)
Falcon Middle School

NOTHING

There's nothing around me, just blackness,
There's nothing to see,
Nothing to hear,
I'm walking into nothing.

There's nothing to feel,
Nothing to smell.
Where am I?
I can't tell.

No matter how far I go,
There's still nothing.
I've walked for hours on end,
It's still black, still nothing.

Somebody help me,
Get me out.
It's black, it's cold,
I don't want to be here.

Nobody is coming,
I'm stuck here forever.
No birds, no flowers,
Just black, black, *black!*

Rachel Marshall (10)
Falcon Middle School

NOTHING

I'm trying to think of something,
But I'm not sure what.
I've just had something in my head
And now it's disappeared.
My page is blank,
I don't know what to do.

My mum is cross and dad is mad,
And the dog is dancing round and round,
I don't know why they're doing it.
Brain messages passing through
When I haven't got a clue.

There is nothing in my head,
I'm very tired and going to bed.
I wake up in the morning,
And on the desk there is a poem -
About nothing.

Amorette Perkins (9)
Falcon Middle School

NOTHING

There's nothing in my head
And nothing in my dreams.
There's nothing in my room
And nothing in my house.

There's got to be somewhere
That isn't full of nothing.
But there's nothing in my universe
And nothing in my school,
Not even anything in my best friend's house.

I'm just stuck in a blank world forever,
Help me!
Please!
Hello?

Luke Bamber (10)
Falcon Middle School

NOTHING

I am staring at darkness,
It feels as if nothing's there.
I crawl out of bed
And take my time!

I am staring at darkness,
I wonder if everything's there.
I feel for my desk
But I am only touching the bare space.

I am staring at darkness,
I don't think anything is here at all.
I delicately feel around for my bed
And now that's gone!

I am staring out of the window
Oh! I can see the sun,
I do hope everything will come back
Because the day has just begun.

I am staring at darkness,
I can't think what's happening.
I feel for my desk, phew, it's there,
Then I realise that the nothingness has gone.

Danielle Gosling (10)
Falcon Middle School

Nothing

I'm trying to write a poem
But there's nothing in my head
There's nothing in my room
And there's nothing in my brain.

I don't know what to write
My heart is beating faster
There is darkness surrounding me
I want to get away from here.

All I can hear is my heart pumping
There's nothing around me
There's nothing in my dreams;
It's an awful nightmare.

Nothing here,
Nothing there,
Nothing anywhere.

Josie Steward (9)
Falcon Middle School

NOTHING

My thoughts have been washed away,
There's nothing in my head,
I can't think of anything,
What shall I do?
Please help me.

My brain has stopped working,
I'm in a world of darkness,
Is it all a dream?
I'm in an empty room,
Darkness is all around me.

Ryan Roberts (9)
Falcon Middle School

NOTHING

I want to write a poem,
But there's nothing in my head.
There's nothing on the landing
And there's nothing in my bed.

This nothingness gives me the creeps,
My ears can't hear a thing,
Not even the sound of a passing car,
Not church bells that usually ring.

I want to get away from here,
But there's nothing here, but nothing,
It's like an awful nightmare,
Only it's the real thing.

Chloe Thompson (9)
Falcon Middle School

NOTHING

Monday morning poetry,
I don't know what to write,
My head is twirling
And I want to go home to bed.

Tuesday morning singing,
My notes are muddled up,
I don't know what the words are,
I'm surprised I'm not sent out.

Wednesday morning division,
I can't think how to add,
What, oh what does that sign mean?
I don't even dare to ask.

Thursday morning PE,
I'm struggling with the ropes,
It's as if I'm daydreaming,
What's that we've got to do?

Friday morning science,
I really need some help,
But that teacher's droning on,
She's talking about nothing.

Eleanor Wynne (9)
Falcon Middle School

Nothing

I'm standing in an empty room,
All the toys have been broken.
My PlayStation games as so, so old,
Even my grandad understands them.

My brother's outside in the wet,
My dad's asleep in bed,
My mum's in the kitchen as usual,
While I lie here feeling dead!

I'm watching all the videos in the house,
I've searched in the cupboards for food,
I've played on the dance mat so many times
That my feet are starting to ache.

A marvellous feeling invades my head,
A splendid idea indeed,
Instead of doing 'nothing' . . .
I'll do 'nothing' with someone else!

Louise Slade (9)
Falcon Middle School

NOTHING

My head is feeling hollow
So I'm banging it like a drum,
I suppose I could write about fruit
Like an apple, a pear or a plum.

I can't think what to write
So I guess there is not much point
In writing about
My good old elbow joint.

My head is feeling empty,
My brain is definitely blank,
Wait, I've been writing a poem,
A poem about nothing.

So I've got my brain back!

Abigail Gurney-Read (9)
Falcon Middle School

Nothing

There's really nothing to say,
I mean, not anything really happens,
No excitement, no adventures,
Nothing to be heard of.

All of a sudden I start to ponder
About what I don't know,
I wonder if it was about something in my head,
So that nothing ever happens.

Now I'm truly stuck what to put,
Nothing springs to mind,
Nothing, nothing, nothing.

Jennifer Wicklund (9)
Falcon Middle School

NOTHING!

I'm trying to write a poem,
But all I get is nothing.

There's nothing to inspire me,
So all I get is nothing.

It's midnight, there's no movement,
Absolutely nothing.

Time doesn't seem to be anywhere,
Still, I have nothing.

My poem isn't going very far,
My page is still empty, nothing.

I wake up in the middle of English,
An empty page in front of me, nothing!

Bonita Davies (10)
Falcon Middle School

Nothing

I'm surrounded by nothing,
There's nowhere to go,
No one to have a word with
And no games to play.

I don't know what's going on,
Everything has changed,
All I see is complete black,
There's nothing to do.

My brain is full of nothing,
I can't think at all,
I've got a hole in my head
And we have to write.

There's no one to ask anywhere
For a bit of help,
There's just not a lot to do
And I'm still thinking.

I have lots of things to do
And I know what to write,
I can now talk to my friends,
Everything is fine.

Emma Mulley (10)
Falcon Middle School

NOTHING

Nothing in my room,
Nothing on my bed,
Nothing on the TV,
Nothing in my head.

No one in the lounge,
No one on the loo,
No one in the kitchen,
They've all gone to the zoo.

Nothing in my fridge,
Nothing in my tummy,
Nothing in the oven,
Please feed me Mummy!

Back from the zoo
And I'm getting thinner,
Did you go to the shops?
I want my dinner!

Daisy Conway (9)
Falcon Middle School

NOTHING

There is nothing I can think of,
I'm in a black place,
A vast empty space enlarges my mind,
Everything is disappearing,
In front of my weary eyes,
It feels as if there is nothing left in the world,
Soon I am floating in a pitch-black sky,
Full of glittering stars that gloat their way by
The world has disappeared.
My mind has been cleared,
My body starts to vanish,
I start to panic.
There is nothing left of me,
All that I can hear is my voice echo.
The breezes start to quieten down
And slowly stop,
And so do I.

Charmaine Jermany (9)
Falcon Middle School

My Friend's Pet

My friend's pet is a cat.
My friend's pet cat is a Siamese.
She is a playful cat
And loves to play with feathers.
She's a female cat.
She's got a slim body
And she sleeps in a comfy bed by the radiator.
She loves her food.
She is always a happy cat
And is always careful.
She has blue eyes
And a brown mouth
And brown paws.
She is short until she stretches
And her best food is KiteKat.
She has had tiny kittens.
She is a blue point Siamese
And she is a pretty cat.
She has a nice home
And can wander in the house.
She nicks food from the kitchen.
She likes to be hugged
And I can't wait to see her again.

Jade Cutter (9)
Garvestone CP School

MY PET CAT

My pet is a cat,
Her name is Squiggly Worm.
Sometimes she likes to play
And sometimes she scratches my thumb.
She likes to sleep all day and catch mice at night,
She chases them around the house at night
And plays with them till morning is light.
The cat is sick over the kitchen floor
And why do I always have to clean it up?
It's such a bore.
She really has twitching whiskers
And colours all over her back.
She sits on my lap.
She likes to play chase with newspapers and pencils
And pulls the mat and tears the paper that I put on her back.

Rachel Satchell (8)
Garvestone CP School

My Dog Jack

I have a dog named Jack,
He's small and has brown patches on his back.
He's a Jack Russell and makes a lot of racket.
He's sweet and cute, my little boy.
He loves to play with his toys,
As his ball makes a lot of noise.
One ear up and one ear down
He chases his tail round and round.
He loves his treats,
Bones and biscuits and all types of meats.
He has a wet nose
And loves to pose for my camera.
That's my dog Jack.

Kerrie Farnan (9)
Garvestone CP School

Carry On Poem

I am Jack, I don't like being made fun of.
I am an insult, I like being mean.
I am sometimes mean, I come from the bully.
I am the bully, I like being mean.
I am Jack, I hate the stupid bully.
I am the fight that both of them started.
I am the fist that bruised Jack's eye.
I am Jack's eye, I am closed up tight.
I am Jack, I wish he hadn't done that . . . *ow!*
I am the bully, I am satisfied with my damage.
I am Jack, I am not doing that again.

I am the moral: *Fighting does not pay.*

Jack Pout (9)
Garvestone CP School

DINNER

The calm sweeping motion
Of the big hungry barn owl
Continues despite the rumbling sound of the old tractor,
Squeaks are heard from the over-grown water meadow.
The little mice don't have a chance,
The owl spots the flashes of fur,
Then he has them for dinner.
The scared mice regroup again,
Five faces peep out of the nearest house,
The golden-coloured bird
Raises quite a sight
And stays there to the last minute of light.
The beautiful sight went home
To rest for his early morning flight,
He had finished dining for the rest of the night.

Edward J King (11)
Garvestone CP School

My Geckos

My geckos
in their tank
are my special pets.
My geckos
are black and yellow,
v-shaped dots on their heads.
My geckos
do not eat very much,
just a cricket now and again!
My geckos are very timid.

My geckos wink at me.
My geckos can dig.
My geckos hide
under the rocks.
I love my geckos.

Toby Allerton (9)
Garvestone CP School

I Never Saw It Again

The owl came swooping down early in the morning,
It landed on my window sill
And gave me a wake up call.
It was brown and white
With little black specks on its silk white chest.
The sun was shining beautiful and bright,
It was golden yellow
And the owl was my little fellow.
His eyes flickered in the sunlight
And they flashed in the moonlight.
It sat there quietly.
Its enormous eyes were fixed on me
As if I were a ghost.
Suddenly I made a noise,
It flew away and I never saw it again.

Amanda Armiger (11)
Garvestone CP School

My Brother

I have a brother, whose age is two,
Who has lovely blond hair and blue eyes too.

He has a chubby little face and a little round tummy,
When he sees food he thinks, *yummy.*

He is quite tall and has a little round bum.
His hands are sweet, he is lots of fun.

He has a cheeky smile and he loves Polos.
He's a mischievous monkey wherever he goes.

He has lots of teeth which he cleans every day.
He gives you cuddles and now he does say,

Mummy, Daddy and brother too, K-K for Kayleigh,
Co-co for me, his sister, Nanny, Grandad and me!

So now you know my little brother, all cute, cuddly and sweet.
I'll just tell you one more thing, he really is quite neat.

Chloe Myhill (11)
Garvestone CP School

The Robber

If a robber dressed in black jumped out behind my door
I'd kick and scream, of that I would make sure.
I would kick him in the bum
And run downstairs to my mum,
Because if he's extremely thick
He'd fall over and hit his head on a brick.
I would not help him at all
Because he would have a mighty big fall.
I wouldn't feel sorry at all
Especially if he was fat or tall.
I'd tug him out by his long hair,
He most likely wouldn't think it was fair.
I would call the police to catch him
Even though he's fairly thin.
He would get put in prison
And would hate the ghosts that have risen.
The ghosts would have chains that clank and rattle
And smash him around the head with a piece of metal
And then they'd walk into their bodies.

Christopher Farnan (11)
Garvestone CP School

WINTER'S DAY

On a winter's day
You get presents from Santa,
Make snowmen
And have lots of fun.

On a winter's day
You make angels in the snow
And have snowball fights
With your best friends.

On a winter's day
You play lots of games
And spend time with
Your family.

Kayleigh Pollen (8)
Garvestone CP School

My Noisy Animals

The cats are scatty,
The dogs are jumping up,
The guinea pigs are squeaking,
The bird is chirping,
Rabbits are twitching their whiskers.
Me and my mum
Have to feed the animals,
We feed the cats on biscuits,
Dogs on meat,
Guinea pigs on cucumber,
Birds on seeds
And rabbits on grass!
It's driving me crazy.

Sophie Butler (7)
Garvestone CP School

Pip

Pip is a sausage dog,
She sees everything she likes,
She's brown and black
And barks at kites.

She loves pork pies
And chasing my teddy.
She chews on bones
And then she's ready - to run!

Pip is my dog,
I feed her every day.
Once she ate a fish hook,
I am very sorry to say!

Sam Harding (8)
Garvestone CP School

LIGHTS

The sky is inky
With the moon a-glowing
And the sun sparkling
With a twinkling light.
The stars are glittering
In the sky so dirty.
Down in a house
I can see
A lovely shining night light.
In the street
I can see
The flashing street lights.
In another house
I can see
The lovely, dazzling
Christmas lights
Through the snow.

Eleanor Doe (8)
Garvestone CP School

My Family

Families are kind and helpful,
My mum's a kind person,
My dad's funny and kind.
My brothers do naughty things sometimes,
If they started fighting
I would stop them,
Or they would start doing it to me.
My granny helps me knit
So nicely,
It is really good.
My granny is friendly
And really kind.
My uncle is funny
And makes me laugh.
My uncle's dog is cute
It eats anything you give her.
My other uncle
Is really special.
My auntie is good at choosing presents
For Christmas.
Their two dogs are nice too,
One is big
And one is small.

Sara King (7)
Garvestone CP School

My Cat

I'm jumping up,
I see my cat,
My mum comes in
And starts to shout,
'Tidy your room at once!' she cries.
But my cat miaows loud
And I shoo her out!

Marcus Meredith (7)
Garvestone CP School

Who Am I?

I have a big black tum,
I have a big green bum,
With a scaly red tail,
I have sharp, sharp teeth,
Will you smell my breath?
Can you feel my heat?
I am covered in jewels
I have a love for meat
The meat that I eat is pig, lamb, cow, pheasant.

Who am I?
I am a dragon.

Cassandra Carroll (10)
Garvestone CP School

Me And My Friend

Me and my friend
Went for a walk,
So excited,
So delighted
We're going on holiday together!
I can't wait,
Can you?
What are we going to eat?
Well I don't know,
Maybe we'll eat horrible things
Let me think
I want to go now
No matter what
I just want to go!

Hollie Clegg (7)
Garvestone CP School

BEACHES

I like beaches, they're really nice,
I like the sand oozing in my toes.
The water's cold, I like swimming in it.
I like climbing the dunes,
I like rolling down them.
The reeds tickle me.
I like building high sandcastles.
My sister and her friends like it too.
I like water skiing, I like skiing doubles.
The seaweed's slimy,
It feels horrible while I am swimming.
When I am drying myself from swimming
The sand sticks to me.
I like the mud squelching through my toes
When I am walking in it.

Laura Wilkinson (8)
Gresham Village School

Sweets Are Such A Treat

Sweets are such a treat
They whizz me off my feet,
I shouldn't eat too many
Or I'll get a horrid belly.
Some are sweet and some are sour
But most of all I like the ones
Which have lots of fizzy power.

Holly Wright (10)
Gresham Village School

SKIING

Skiing is fun,
Skiing is cool,
This is what I do,
Whizzing through the snow,
The wind in my hair,
Bumping over moguls,
Shooting through the air.
When the wind is bitter
You have to ski quicker.
When the sun is shining
I take my time.
Skiing is fun,
Skiing is cool.

Clare Sampson (9)
Gresham Village School

SMUDGE

I have a rabbit in a hutch
And I love him so very much.

I give him all the best of grub
Just before he has a rub.

His fur is soft, his ears are long,
But sometimes he makes a nasty pong.

He bounds around night and day
And makes his bed in a nest of hay.

He's brown and black with a speck of white,
He looks so sweet when I hold him tight.

Smudge is my very best friend,
Although he drives me round the bend.

Natalie Kinsley (9)
Gresham Village School

FIREWORKS DISPLAY

Fireworks at night
Always give me a fright.
Bang, whee, whizz, pop!
Off they go,
Told you so . . .
Ah, that's better, quiet at last.

Florence Blyth (9)
Gresham Village School

THE ISLAND

T is for trees swaying in the breeze.
H is for beach huts shading you from the dazzling sun.
E is for eagerness of the children running to the sea.

I is for the ice cream in any flavour you want.
S is for suncream covering you in a layer of protection.
L is for lying all day long tanning and relaxing.
A is for apples, they are so boring, have a pineapple or a coconut.
N is for nothing, that's just what you can do.
D is for doubt, you will never have it because you're in paradise.

Grace Blakesley-Park (10)
Gresham Village School

ANIMALS!

A ll the alligators accelerated with anticipation alarmingly
into some anteaters but automatically apologised.
N ine newts nibbling nuts and Neapolitan ice cream
while nattering nonsense about New Zealand.
I nfinite, impossible iguanas interrupting some
imaginative ibis while indulging in insects.
M any magnificent and mischievous monkeys misbehaving
themselves and muttering maliciously about mongooses.
A s the adventurous and athletic antelope did aerobics with attitude
the apprehensive ants watched in admiration.
L ots of livid leopards living luxuriously in Lapland
and licking ice lollies.
S eventeen sinister and sophisticated salamanders
showing off their splendid and sparkly stilettos.

Christobel Hastings-Knowles (10)
Gresham Village School

If You Want To See A Tiger

If you want to see a tiger
You must go through the dark,
Dark jungle.

I know a tiger
Who's living down there,
He's a fierce one, he's a tough one,
He's wicked and he's . . . hungry.

Yes, if you really want to see a tiger
You must go through, I repeat, go through
The dark, dark jungle.

Go down the muddy hill and say,
'Here tiger! Here tiger!
Here tigerrrrrr!'

And out he'll come
But don't stand there too long,
Run! Run! Run!

Sophie Regis (8)
Gresham Village School

The Row

My eyes are sore,
I feel so bad,
My head is throbbing,
My cheeks are stinging.

My eyes are sore,
Tears are slowly travelling through my skin.
I hear *them* shouting loudly,
I wish my mum was holding me in her arms,
I wish this was all part of a dream.

My eyes are sore,
The shouting has stopped,
I finally come out,
My mum hugs me,
I feel happy.

Chris Robertson (9)
Old Catton Middle School

My Cat Coco

I could hear his purr in my head.
When I watched TV
I could feel his paws on my lap.
I feel sick because it was not my fault.
I will never forget him.

I could hear his purr in my head.
I used to play with him at night.
He used to curl up on my bed
When I was asleep.

I could hear his purr in my head.
His tail used to curl up my leg.
He used to put his paw in the pond.
I loved him.

Zoe Rushmer (9)
Old Catton Middle School

Sitting On My Bed

I'm sitting on my bed . . . then . . .
I'm bowling for England at number ten
With crowds cheering me on.
I'm swimming with lilac dolphins
In the deep blue sea.
I'm battling a stripy tiger in the jungle.

I'm sitting on my bed . . . then . . .
I'm watching colourful butterflies
In my garden dancing
Around the swaying flowers.
I'm playing football for Arsenal . . .
For the FA Cup.
I'm racing a train in my new BMW.

Liam Waller (9)
Old Catton Middle School

Oh My Grandad

My tears bring memories to my mind.
I feel like he's by my side.
I wish he was here but he has died.
Oh my grandad.

My tears bring memories to my mind.
How I miss you.
I want you here by my side.
When I think of you it makes me cry.
Oh my grandad.

My tears bring memories to my mind.
How I miss you
But the past's behind.
Oh my grandad.

My tears bring memories to my mind.
I'll try to forget the pain in my mind.
I'll try to remember you all my life.
Oh my grandad.

My tears bring memories to my mind.
How I miss you.
I'll think of you always.
Oh my grandad.

Shalini Vallepur (9)
Old Catton Middle School

A Crying Situation

The mane of my heart begins to melt
When I've done something wrong.
I run upstairs scared and afraid,
Worried and down.
Nobody cares.

The mane of my heart begins to melt.
I have a feeling inside me like a disturbing fright.
My face gets red and hot not cold.
The night scares when I cry.
My sulk carries on for a minute or more.

The mane of my heart begins to melt
In falling life when I cry.
My eyes sulk minute by minute
That's a crying situation.

Kirsten Hamilton (8)
Old Catton Middle School

Colours

Orange is a varnished chair.
Purple is a tin of beetroot, a throne in a golden palace,
Cherries on a tree.
Pink is a rose in the garden, a happy day.
Blue is the sky, Eeyore's beautiful face reflected in the water.
Green is the winter garden all lit up,
The grass on a glamorous, glazing day.
Gold is rings on a wedding day, the christening of a baby.
Red is a vampire's teeth dripping with blood.

Savannah Colclough (9)
Old Catton Middle School

DAYDREAMING

I close my eyes
I'm bouncing through the fluffy white clouds
On a springy, fuscia trampoline.
I'm diving from the steepest diving board
Into an ice-cold pool.
I'm swinging through the jungle
On slippery silver vines
Listening to the sounds
Of ferocious animals.

Briony Howarth (9)
Old Catton Middle School

Fireside

The hot flames
are shooting up the chimney
like an erupting volcano.
They are a cat licking the wood
ready to eat.
They are Jack's beanstalk
climbing up towards the sky.
Kangaroos jumping across
the Australian plains.

The wood is a prisoner
being tortured for information.

The iron grate is a torture chamber
hidden in the wall.
A goblin's dungeon deep down
in the caverns under the Earth.

The hearth is a passageway down
to a cave full of treasure.

The embers are caterpillars
crawling across a leaf.

Alison Jones (9)
Old Catton Middle School

DAYDREAMING

I close my eyes,
I'm a forest
or pink glistening plums
dangling on the lowest and highest branches
of glinting trees.

I'm in a bright world of fairy tales
in the happy land.

I'm in the deep huge land of the ocean
swirling and twirling like a mermaid.

I'm in the wind with a soft breeze
washing gently around me.

Danielle Collins (9)
Old Catton Middle School

THE FIRESIDE

The flames are orange juice pouring into a cup of ice cubes.
The sparks are fire ants crawling to keep hot.
The logs are brown paint, when Mark poured too much,
They are chocolate ice cream, dribbling orange sauce.
The sound is my mum's wonderful cooking sizzling in the oven.
It is cold water splashed into a boiling, spitting pan.
The black grate is the Chamber of Secrets from Harry Potter.
The orange embers are a wizard's mixing potion.
The ash is a black night with sparks for stars.

Sam Eastop (9)
Old Catton Middle School

DAYDREAMING

Teacher thinks I'm listening
But I'm not.

I'm sitting in the shoe shop
Buying some shoes.
Red, pink, blue shoes
Which ones shall I choose?

I'm standing in the clothes shop
Staring at a dress,
Trying to work out
Which one looks best.

I'm playing my trumpet in the park
After dark.
My fans are shouting,
'Wicked!'

Charlotte Lorraine (9)
Old Catton Middle School

THE WINTER'S COLD . . .

The snowy white blanket of snow across the lonely land
Like Jack Frost has been and gone,
A sparkling pile of feathers,
The lakes are frozen ice, quiet and still,
Icicles hanging like a party hat upside down.

The cold snow has come and sprinkled the ground with white,
The whistling wind racing like a rally car
And the breeze replies every day like a question with 100 answers!

The neighbours all start to weep,
Nobody in the town could sleep,
It was all a mystery,
The whole town thinks that the cold should go away.

The shivering cold, he would not go away
And by morning he refused again like a pop star not doing
as they're told,
Filling the land, the cold he does,
Sprinkling snowflakes, like crisps out of the bag.

The land was crying of coldness,
With the snow-dropped trees hanging still
And the people of the town still weeping . . .

Amy Collins (10)
Poringland Primary School

The Winter's Cold

The freezing cold has invited Jack Frost
Like an invitation to a party in the lonely land.
With frosty icicles all around and crunchy lakes
Like a Christmas mad house of snow.

All around Jack has visited for whistling winds are also here
Like an army has come to attack with spiky winds
Of thick, pure white snow.

It's making people cry with despair, for it's numbing their bodies
Like a snowman melting, but melting because of the cold.
People wrap up warm with scarves, gloves and hats
Like they're ready for a skiing trip.

Ducks are sliding and skating all over the lakes
Like they're in a competition on a real ice skating ring,
But not quite like professionals!
And all nature is hibernating and birds are migrating.

The land cries for the warmth, for everything is snow.
Icicles hanging dangerously about to chip off
Like leaves falling in winter.

Helena Norman (9)
Poringland Primary School

THE WINTER'S COLD

On the freezing cold land
The whistling wind sails across the horizon
Like a boat on the high seas.
The cold, he sprinkles blankets of snow
All over the world.

The cold, he comes again,
His ghostly white face,
His sharp, shivering features piercing.

People are freezing, the numbness is here,
They trudge through the crunchy snow
Like the motion of small teeth
Sinking into a deep apple.

'Make us cold no longer,' cries the land,
'For we have died a beautiful death
But we will live again.'

Naomi Carter (10)
Poringland Primary School

THE BLEAK WEATHER

As the people sniff on a hazy night
And pelicans curl up so as not to perish,
The rabbits observe some headlights
Like a boy consuming his big dish.
While the bitter night gets more nippy
The families decide to huddle and curl,
As the deer stares strongly at the slush below
And the babies breathe out and watch it whirl.

Frost is settling on the ground and grass
Like some people's lips cracking,
As the polar bear travels for food
And the seagull to keep warm is flying.
As the crisp ground needs underground heat
Foxes snuggle up in their burrows
And the eel is swimming in its depth
As the raging river rapidly flows.

Andrew Todd (10)
Poringland Primary School

On This Perishing Night

On this perishing night we quiver,
Between the plants a stoat does slither.
A rabbit and hare stop and stare
Like a statue of the Queen.

Frost settles on the ground
Like a heavy blanket coming down.
Sheep flock together on the hillside
Whilst the owl ogles onward at its prey.

But stags shiver, shaking with fear
As midnight draws very near.
Families snuggle together in the warm
Like a huddle of penguins in Antarctica.

In the snow hares make no sound
Like robbers breaking out.
The powerful icy wind makes you shiver,
On this perishing night we quiver.

Charlie Newman (11)
Poringland Primary School

THE WINTER COLD

The freezing white snow, the sparkling snow,
The ice-striped snow, Jack Frost has come for the winter.
The snow covered wasteland is like a cloud,
Like a snowy blanket.

The winter has come, the snow has come,
From the sky snow drifts down to the ground
Like a feather from a pillow up high.

The town's people get a cold from the snow,
With their red faces and blowing their noses,
The cold keeps them awake shivering and shaking,
They wake up to more snow in the morning.

The shivering sheep get sprinkles on their wool,
The cowering dogs in the house,
The badgers are hibernating in their home,
The birds are flying south.

The snow covers the land, melting away,
Down the hills and down the fields,
Back to the icy river.

Thomas Morris (10)
Poringland Primary School

THE WINTER'S COLD

In the cold, Jack Frost sprinkled his frost
Onto a snowy cold blanket.
The lonely land has sprinkled, snow-dropped trees.
The silver moon slightly droops.

Whistling winds whoosh past.
The howling wind shivering,
Making ghostly white faces.

Numbing fingers, faces shades of blue,
Wrap up warm.
Losing your breath and fresh pink faces.

Ducks sliding across icy waters.
Animals cuddling up for hibernation.
Rabbits' fur sprinkled with snow.
Birds curled up together.

Lands crying of coldness.
Icicles hanging from houses.
A smooth snowy blanket is seen for miles.

Laura Utting (10)
Poringland Primary School

The Winter's Cold

In a freezing cold land
The ice is slippery and the snow is cold
Like a huge freezer.
Jack Frost has come and made all things white
And he jumps around like a plane on its flight.

The cold has come as white as a ghost
Whilst he's bringing snow and ice,
Like a sparkling message from afar.

The people are freezing, the numbness is here,
They trudge through the crunchy snow
Like the motion of small teeth
Sinking into a deep apple.

The deer are running to get to their homes
To start hibernating 'til the winter goes,
Like people in houses
And the eggs in their nest.

'Make us cold no longer,' cries the land,
'For we have died a beautiful death
But we will live again.'

Ben Lambert (10)
Poringland Primary School

My Scary Brother

When I am asleep at night
My brother puts on the light,
I think he's a knight
When he stands in the moonlight.

My brother has got bushy eyebrows,
My brother wakes up,
His hair sticks up like points.

His eyes are scary,
His body is shimmering
Like tin in the moonlight.

Craig Turner (9)
St Michael's VA Middle School

Storm

Lights out, power cut,
Fork lightning shoots down from the sky,
Cats and dogs howling in their huts
Awhooooo.
Parents and children sit in their houses
Eating their mince pies!

Bethany Howard (9)
St Michael's VA Middle School

All About My Dog

He loves me when I cry,
He comforts me when I sigh,
    That's my dog.
He likes running in the fog,
He likes Miss Hogg,
    That's my dog.

Lucy Bezants (9)
St Michael's VA Middle School

BETH GELERT

Llewellyn went out hunting
And it had been a bad day,
Cos he did not catch anything
And he lost his way.

The baby boy was sleeping,
A wolf came through the door,
Beth Gelert went fighting
And the wolf wanted more.

The wolf dropped down dead,
Beth Gelert was a hero
And the baby was still in bed,
Beth Gelert gave him a right old tero.

Llewellyn ran through the door
And he had a fright,
Seeing all the blood on the floor
And it was nearly night.

Llewellyn scant round for his baby,
He stabbed his faithful friend,
He thought that he killed his baby maybe,
He saw his baby round the bend.

He looked at his dead dog,
He's glad his baby is OK,
He buried him near a log
And you can see his dog from this day.

Georgia Heggie (10)
St Michael's VA Middle School

THE MAGIC BOX

(Based on 'Magic Box' by Kit Wright)

I will put in the box . . .

An angel's sweet smile,
A glittering star glowing in the sky,
A sweet baby's laugh.

I will put in the box . . .

The whistle of a man,
A curl from my mum's hair,
A golden ring glowing in the dark.

I will put in the box . . .

A mermaid swimming in the shining sea,
A sun as black as the sky,
Yellow as the sun.

My box is made from gold and petals
With feathers from a golden bird
And secrets hiding in a corner.

In my box I will . . .

Swim with the dolphins under the waves,
Play with my favourite friend,
Ride a horse in the dark sky.

Ebony Barber (9)
St Michael's VA Middle School

Raindrop

Clash, rattle, clatter and crackle,
Rumble goes the day.
Crash, bang, boom, dackle
The storm will fade away.

Boom, bang, whoosh, splash,
The cat is getting wet.
Drip, drop, plip, pash
I bet my pet is wet!

Lisa Manning (10)
St Michael's VA Middle School

The Graveyard

A graveyard can be scary,
It is a peaceful place,
There are all different headstones
With lots of different names,
It can look very pretty
With lots of different flowers,
The children's area is very sad,
Kites, windmills blowing in the air,
Doesn't make me feel so sad.

Kate Lemmon (10)
St Michael's VA Middle School

Life

Life is red,
Life is bad,
Life stays in bed,
Life is sad,
Life is to give,
Life is fun,
It is given to you like you're its son,
Life is good,
Don't cut it down like a lump of wood,
Don't waste it.

Naomi Gray (11)
St Michael's VA Middle School

LEEDS UNITED

L eeds United Football Club.
E very time we win a match
E very member of the team cheers.
D o you think we'll win the league?
S coring goals is our task.

U nder pressure every match.
N o goals scored by the other team.
I n our goal stands Paul Robinson,
T eaching the other teams a lesson.
E very game the other team are in tears.
D o you think we'll win the cup?

Matthew Tickle (10)
St Michael's VA Middle School

My Doberman, Max

I've got a Doberman,
He's black and tan.
His name is Max,
His brother's Sam.
They run together every day,
They run and chase the birds away.
They run together rain or shine,
Boy am I glad this dog is mine.
I love my dog,
He's loyal and true,
A man's best friend,
I now know.

Kirsty Swatman (11)
St Michael's VA Middle School

Me And My Pets

Me and my pets are quiet happy
And one is called Mr Snappy.
He is a rabbit
And has dirty habits
That I hate a lot!

Me and my pets are quite normal
And one is called Miss Snormal.
She is a parrot
Who only eats carrots
That I hate a lot!

Me and my pets are quite silly,
Just like Mr and Mrs Lilly.
Both of them are guinea pigs,
Both are tall and both are big,
That I hate a lot!

Amy Clarke (10)
St Michael's VA Middle School

POETRY

P uzzling and perplexing,
O rdinary and opinionated,
E scalating and executive,
T op and talented,
R esourceful and respected,
Y ee hah!

Kevin Browne (11)
St Michael's VA Middle School

I'M FRIGHTENED

I'm frightened
That you'll run away.
I'm frightened
That you'll leave.
I'm frightened
That there's not enough
For you and I to achieve.
I'm frightened
That you'll scream, punch and kick,
But most of all I'm frightened
Because I love until I'm sick.

John Chapman (10)
St Michael's VA Middle School

A Poem Of Me

J essica is my name,
E xciting things I do,
S ewing I like,
S ums in maths is fun,
I ce cream I like to eat,
C lumsy sometimes
A nd a good actress I am.

M aths I like,
C razy I can be,
G ood at looking after people that are hurt or ill,
E ating McDonald's I do sometimes,
E njoying things around.

Jessica McGee (10)
St Michael's VA Middle School

If Everyone Was Friends!

If everyone was friends the world would be a better place,
Everyone would get on, whatever race,
If terrorism did not exist
We would all hug and kiss.

If everyone was friends we would have more fun,
Playing and running in the sun,
No one would stop us
And kick up a fuss.

If everyone was friends everything would be fair
And we would all be willing to share,
We would all be as one,
We would never be alone.

If everyone was friends life would not be about war,
There would be no evil behind that door,
Life would not be about teasing,
It would be about pleasing.

If everyone was friends there would be no evil,
No one would know about the Devil
Who has stopped us from getting along,
When we all know together we are strong.

If everyone was friends the world would be a better place,
We all know we want our own equal space,
We all want to be as one,
So why is nothing going to be done?

Mark Asker (11)
St Michael's VA Middle School

Valentine's Day!

Messages of love
From ear to ear,
Presents and gifts
To give and receive.

Notes of love
In many different ways,
Writing and giving
But always nice to hear.

Expressions of love,
A very kind thought,
Words and letters,
It's always nice to know.

Nicola Whiley (11)
St Michael's VA Middle School

HATE

Hate is an arrow
Like a poisoned spear,
Haunting like darkness
He's ever so near,
Tiptoes at midnight,
Steals your heart,
As sharp as a dagger,
An inescapable dart,
He's as real as can be,
He's not a deception,
He's hunting you down,
There are no exceptions,
He whispers a curse
Under his breath,
There is no escape,
As traumatic as death,
He blacks out the sun,
Darkness will rule,
Heart turned to black,
Blood a dark pool,
Hate is an arrow
Like a poisoned spear,
Haunting like darkness
He's ever so, ever so, ever so *near!*

Nicole Dyke (10)
St Michael's VA Middle School

THE LISTENERS 2

As his horse trooped through the forest
The traveller looked round,
Everything was still, nothing moved,
Nothing made a noise, no whisper or a sound.

But little did he know something was lurking,
There was strangeness in the air,
A creature in the forest had awakened
And was moving in its lair.

A pair of eyes looked through the trees,
His sword was by his side,
Feeling it with careful hands
His braveness was denied.

The traveller had reached his goal,
The forest edge was near
But suddenly the creature emerged,
He was struck with fear.

The horse went wild with worry
As the wolf jumped out with surprise,
The traveller raised his crossbow,
The rooster called sunrise.

The traveller shot a bolt
Right at the wolf's leg,
The wolf went whimpering off
Back to its bed.

Liam Ross (11)
St Michael's VA Middle School

THE MAGIC BOX

(Based on 'Magic Box' by Kit Wright)

I will put in the box . . .

A munching of giraffes in the long trees,
An elephant washing with sparkling water,
A rabbit hopping with joy in the garden.

I will put in the box . . .

The darkest, spookiest forest with howling wolves,
A golden, glistening horse galloping upon the sand,
Dancing bluebells waving in the wind.

My box is fashioned with glowing stars,
With blue and purple hearts and silver ribbon.

I will meet a famous artist in my box
And paint with Van Gogh.

Antonia Beck (9)
St Michael's VA Middle School

The Zoo

On my visit to the zoo
I met a baby monkey,
He was cuddly and cute,
He thought he was funky.

On my visit to the zoo
I met a funny kangaroo,
He was bouncy and lively
And always jumping to the loo.

On my visit to the zoo
I met a well-trained seal,
He was tricky and clever,
He really enjoyed his meal.

On my visit to the zoo
I met a cheetah who was fast,
He ran every day in the sun
And he was never ever last.

Melissa Fewtrell (9)
St Michael's VA Middle School

Stars And Moon

Stars twinkling in the pitch-black sky.
The bright blue morning has become now nigh.
Next to the glowing round moon,
Stars in the air will be gone soon.

Moonbeams making the stars so bright,
Oh! What a big and beautiful sight.
The stars and moon shining on whatever they see,
Including the long and whistling trees.

An owl flying, looking for its prey
And a lonely person wondering what to say.
The glowing stars and moon
Are fading away and will be gone soon.

Leia Barnard (10)
St Michael's VA Middle School

Scooby

He has eyes that glow like an owl,
He snores like a pig at night,
He has spots like a cow
And he plays football like Beckham.

He is as fluffy as a teddy,
He is as playful as people,
He has a brown and white nose,
He lives in a kennel.

He likes to eat his food,
He likes to play with toys,
He likes teddy bears,
He is my puppy!

Arty Draper (10)
St Michael's VA Middle School

My Amazing Goldfish

Bubbles and Barney are my fish,
They love to swim all the time,
They especially love to wish,
They don't like nasty crime.

They normally have sword fights with their tails,
'Scrumptious, scrumptious and scrumptious food,' they say,
They wish they could sail,
They always swim the same kind of way.

Jasmine Crotch (9)
St Michael's VA Middle School

My Dad

He's warm as a pillow
And is cuddlier than my teddy.

My dad has hair like a gorilla,
I love my dad more than ever.

My dad says goodnight, sweet dreams,
I love you and I love you too.

My dad is more caring than ever
And is kinder than ever to me.

Casey Quadling (9)
St Michael's VA Middle School

MILLIE

Millie, she is black like night
You can see her eyes in the light
She growls like a bear
And she can be sweet as a pear
She eats everything
Sometimes they go *ping!*
She follows you around all day
As you know she wants to play
She's fat as a pig
Her tongue is long as a frog's
She's got teeth like a shark's
She bites like a tiger
Her fur is like a teddy bear
Her eyes are like diamonds
She lays like a monkey
Her lips are like velvet
She runs like a cheetah
And that is Millie.

Jack Thorogood (9)
St Michael's VA Middle School

ME!

So sweet I am, old I am not
Pretty as can be, honest - that's certainly me.
I am the one and only,
So shy, I am understanding, that's me
Loveable me, lazy I am certainly not
Volunteer I certainly do not
And I am nice as can be.

Sophie O'Sullivan (11)
St Michael's VA Middle School

My Mestopheles

Mr Mestopheles a sleek, fat, bold cat.
His mingly coloured fur is silky and fluffy.
His eyes glow and twinkle.
A silky, soft, twitchy tail.
Straight flicky, long whiskers.
Spiky, short, soft ears turn.
He scatters nervously then hovers.
He's bone idle and hungry all the time.
Friendly, sleepy and lovely.

Rebecca Windscheffel (9)
St Michael's VA Middle School

The Dude's Nude

There once lived a dude,
Who went to school in the nude.
He went to the head,
And the teacher said,
'How could you be so rude?'

Daniel Tickle (10)
St Michael's VA Middle School

Guinea Pigs!

They're cute,
they're small,
not at all tall.

They squeak,
they eat,
they're not called Pete.

What are they?
My guinea pigs!

They eat vegetables, hay
and they don't even pay!

They hide, they scamper
and they're not a camper.

Who are they?
My guinea pigs!

Kaye Quinn (10)
St Michael's VA Middle School

My Big Brother

My big brother, he's so mean
He also thinks he's king
He messes about all day
He's my big brother.

My big brother, he's a pig
He tries to eat the things I eat
It's a shame he's not got a wig
My big brother, he's so big!

Evie Tansley (9)
St Michael's VA Middle School

My Mother

My mother,
She's very, very kind,
But she's my mum,
She's very warm, cuddly and soft,
But she's my mum,
My mum is very helpful, just like me,
But she's my mum,
She's very kind and caring,
But she's my mum
And all that matters to me is my mum!

Jade Hudson (9)
St Michael's VA Middle School

Mysteries Of The Night

When you're walking down the street
And it's very, very dark
You see the mysteries of the night.
Something moves, was it a ghost or a cat?
You hear something howling, a wolf or a dog?
You're walking down the street, you start to run.
As you hear the mysteries of the night
Did something touch me or was it me?
Something or someone pushes past me,
Silently as it slowly walks past
I feel something wet and hot
Against my leg.
It's my cat Ribbons come to greet me.
From the mysteries of the night.

Poppy Gooding (9)
St Michael's VA Middle School

Harry Potter

I thought I saw a golden snitch,
Oh that's why, it's quidditch.
I really saw Ron,
He offered me a bonbon.
I saw Tom Riddle,
He put me in a fiddle.
I saw Hermione Granger,
Her dad's a park ranger.
I lived in a cupboard under the stairs with doors,
When I went to Hogwarts I was put in Gryffindor.
I saw Ron's sister Ginny,
She drove a small Mini.
I saw Professor Snape,
He wore a Slytherin cape.
I saw a boy in Hufflepuff,
He was tough and rough.
I saw a boy in Ravenclaw
He was petrified on the floor.
In the Gryffindor common room,
Seamus made a spell and went *kaboom!*

Kameron Dawson (10)
St Michael's VA Middle School

My BMX Race

Long drive to the track
And now there's no turning back
My helmet feels like velvet
My gloves I love
I'm at the start gate
I'm on a hill
Riders ready
Can't go slow
Bumps and humps
Clear so near
Bike that people like
I've got to ride fast
If not, I'll be last
When I clear, people stare and they cheer.
The track is long and hard to ride.
My mates are at my side
My mate is in a state
Cos he's going to be late
Our pedals go round
Someone falls to the ground
With excitement and fear
I fly through the air
My legs are like jelly
And I've got butterflies in my belly
I can see the end
As I steer round the bend
I'm number one and I can see my mum
I'm dying of thirst because I'm first.
Got a medal for riding fast pedal.

Jake Klein (9)
St Michael's VA Middle School

David Beckham

David Beckham has great skill,
The ball he easily controls.
He can score from a mile!
He passes the ball with style.
He tries out every style of hair,
The captain's band he wears.
The boots he has are never cheap,
No studs, but blades he wears.
He knows when tacklers are near,
Moves away with speed,
The crowd cheer!

Kyle Cain (9)
St Michael's VA Middle School

About Babies

Babies grow in Mummies' tummies,
Then they pop out into the world.
They cry and scream,
They play with their toys.
They wear tiny baby clothes,
Their mums push them in prams.
Then when they get older,
They go to playschool.

Iain Savage (9)
St Michael's VA Middle School

Best Friends

Friends comfort you if you get hurt,
They'll wipe off every piece of dirt!

Having sleepovers are great fun,
Stay up late, eating a bun!

Birthday parties and all that cake,
Eat so much our tummies ache!

Some days we argue all day long,
But we soon find we've done wrong.

Some holidays I must go away,
But my friend has fun anyway.

Fiona Walls (10)
St Michael's VA Middle School

SWEET DREAMS

In the dark, dark wood I stared and stood,
A shadow shot through the tree,
I wondered, what it could be?
Was it an alien from out of space?
Was it the sunshine showing me his face?

I wish I was brave enough to open my eyes
To see what shadow in the sky
I started to run so quick like a hare in a fix,
My heart thumping, *thud! Thud! Thud!*
A voice shouting me, Reuben it's time to wake up!

Reuben Long (9)
St Michael's VA Middle School

EXCITEMENT

Excitement is orange
And smells of lush green grass.
Excitement tastes like chocolate ice cream.
It sounds like people at the beach.
Excitement is smooth like paper.
It lives in Beano Land.

James Moon (10)
Woodland View Middle School

The Victorian Kitchen

As I walked in, mouth-watering smells came from the oven,
I could catch a whiff of a freshly preserved blackberry jam,
I took a bite of a freshly baked drop scone,
It was warm, squidgy, and ever so delicious,
I love it in the Victorian farmhouse kitchen.

I stepped into the pantry and its hard flagstone floor felt cold on my feet
I felt warm and cosy sitting next to the fire, cooking,
Though the smells wafting about me made me feel so hungry,
I went to the pump to get water for making tea in the copper kettle,
I love it in the Victorian farmhouse kitchen.

In the background I could hear the copper kettle hissing and whistling,
I heard the rain pattering down on the floor outside
and was glad to be inside,
I could hear the fire spitting and crackling,
As I put my saucepan down onto the range it clattered,
I love it in the Victorian farmhouse kitchen.

I look around me and I see the pantry shelves stacked
with currents and flour.
I see the larder packed with meat and diary products,
I see the shelves stacked with preserves and pickles,
I look around and I can't see anything I don't like,
How I love it in the Victorian farmhouse kitchen.

Emma Cooper (10)
Woodland View Middle School

Farmhouse Kitchen Poem

As I sit on my chair I can see a big black stove.
The sound of the sizzling pans makes my tummy rumble.
The feel of the drop scones mixture.
I am making it soft and wet.

My feet are cold as they touch the hard flagstone floor.
I can hear the drip-drop of the water
Dripping from the water pump over the sink.
I can see the steam of the copper kettle.
Oh good, it must be ready.

I take the oil lamp to the pantry to help me see
And I get some jam to have with my supper.
I can hear a squeaking noise as I shut the pantry door,
I hope we haven't got little visitors in there.

Jodie Saunders (10)
Woodland View Middle School

HOPE

Hope is lilac
It smells like roses
Hope tastes like strawberry ice cream
It sounds like birds singing
It feels like a sponge
Hope lives on top of a cloud.

Rebecca Smith (10)
Woodland View Middle School

The Maid

There I was in the wet and cold.
I strolled into the warm and cosy.
Polished the brass and lit the stove.
Down came my lady for her breakfast.

My first job was to wash the floor.
The hard, dirty flagstone floor.
Next to make my lady some tea.
Some strong, sweet tea.

Silence was all I could hear.
Although I could hear the horses near.
The smell of the strong tea.
Over the smell of the burning stove.

Later and later it's getting.
Darker and darker it's becoming.
Time to leave the warm and cosy.
Back to the wet and cold.

The same jobs tomorrow I've been told.

Laura Burroughs (11)
Woodland View Middle School

SOUNDS OF THE FARMHOUSE KITCHEN

Farmhouse kitchen, warm and cosy,
Red and yellow flames
Flickering in the fire,
Leaping from the pitch-black range.

Large copper kettle, battered and worn,
Full of steam hissing and bubbling
Gurgling like a stream,
Steaming on the massive hot stove.

With the smell of dried currants
In the well-stocked pantry,
Shelves of sugar, bottled fruit being preserved,
Water dripping on the hard white sink.

John Taylor (11)
Woodland View Middle School

PICTURES IN MY MIND

Cold and wet outside,
Warm and cosy inside
Warm your hands by the fire.
You'll feel safe in the kitchen.

The cook will make you drop scones,
They taste delicious,
You can help her cook
The potatoes for the farm workers.

You can hear the burning of the fire.
The rain outside hits the windows.
You can hear the animals outside,
You can hear the cook talking to the workers.

As you walk in you can smell the food.
If you go into the larder you can smell the meat.
You can almost smell the warmth.
The drop scones smell good.

The water pump sitting on the sink.
The hard flagstone floor.
The bright flames from the stove.
The flickering oil lamps in the corner.

Evie Warren (11)
Woodland View Middle School

Life In A Farmhouse Kitchen

The kitchen had lots of pots and pans.
On the shelves were shining tin cans.
The kitchen maid worked very hard
To bake the flour and the lard.

Strange meats to cook.
Recipes not out of a book.
Things we don't eat today.
We look forward to fresh vegetables in May.

Pots and pans scrubbed by hand
Are always in demand.
Early risers, up by five.
At the end of the day more dead than alive.

Will Howard (11)
Woodland View Middle School

The Teacher From New York

There was a teacher from New York
Who liked eating a lot of pork,
For he said, 'I'm not fat,'
He exploded like that.
That old fat teacher from New York.

Emma Wilcock (10)
Woodland View Middle School

DEATH

Death is black,
It smells like hot sick.
Death tastes like boiled sprouts,
It sounds like people screaming.
It feels like slimy slugs.
Death lives in the heart of a volcano.

Grace Henshaw (9)
Woodland View Middle School

Farmhouse Kitchen

Standing on the flagstone floor,
I walked through a creaky door,
Into the kitchen room,
Where there was an old lady with a broom.

The old lady was cooking,
Flipping pancakes without looking,
The lady lit the oil lamp,
The match wouldn't light because it was damp.

It was wet and damp out the door,
Just as cold as the flagstone floor,
She washed her hands in the sink,
It was quite cosy, I think.

Lee Chamberlin (11)
Woodland View Middle School

Toasting Guy Fawkes

Remember, remember
The fifth of November
Smoke in my eyes
Because of the skies
Gloomy and dull
Catherine wheels spitting
Showers of sparks
Rockets zooming
Through the air
Traffic lights,
Red, yellow and green
Brightly coloured flames,
Toasting Guy Fawkes
Sparklers make pretty patterns
In the air.
Fluorescent colours come to a halt
Run to the car
And go home
Never to forget this night.

Sarah Brooks (8)
Woodland View Middle School

KENNINGS

A bird snatcher,
A sharp fighter.

Good eyesight,
A mouse killer.

Sharp paws,
Dangerous claws.

A catalogue to
Make a *cat!*

Ethan Morgan (10)
Woodland View Middle School

WINTER POEM

I ran outside to play in the cold, windy, white snow,
I look up at the colourful, icy lights that glow.
I try to see the peaceful hills, wet and light,
I look up at the muffled stars so bright.
I walk up to the trees all bare and dripping,
I look down the rabbit hole and the rabbits are kipping.
I skip to the window the fire burning warm and calm,
Then I hear Mum and Dad's alarm
The wind is blowing hard and clear,
Then I feel a tear.
I hear a hedgehog rushing around,
I see robins cold as can be playing on the ground.
I feel snow so cold and hard, icy hail,
I hear the wind *bang, clang* at the pail.
The sky is grey and black,
Then I hear my pony rattle her tack.
I'm very happy now because it's . . . winter!

Gemma Fricker (9)
Woodland View Middle School

A Snake Kenning

A slithering blob,
A thin log,
A whip lash,
A quick dash,
A shed of skin,
Thicker than a pin,
A hissing song,
A body that's long,
A long shake,
To make me a snake.

Charlotte Stokes (11)
Woodland View Middle School

A Snake Kenning

A colourful carnivore
A slithering slob
A whip lash
A quick dash
A venomous spit
A shedding skin
A catalogue to make me . . .
A snake.

Abbi Finney (11)
Woodland View Middle School

Nature

Grass is green and wild
Like a child
Birds go tweet
So they are sweet
Cats on the garden wall
It makes them look tall
Stars in the midnight sky
To remember the people that die
Sunlight in the morning
Daylight is dawning
I'm glad we have nature.

Grace Edwards (10)
Woodland View Middle School

There Was A Young Kid Of Norwich

There was a young kid of Norwich
Who liked to eat runny porridge.
For he said, 'Dad's is best,
A class above the rest!'
That young porridge kid of Norwich.

James Hale (10)
Woodland View Middle School

There Was A Santa From The North Pole

There was a Santa from the North Pole
Who was so overweight he could roll.
For he said, 'If I fall
I would roll like a ball,'
That Santa who was from the North Pole.

Eleanor Mills (10)
Woodland View Middle School

The Farmhouse Kitchen

In the farmhouse kitchen,
There is a big black stove,
In the farmhouse kitchen,
The floor is hard and cold,
In the farmhouse kitchen,
The larder is cool and dark.

In the farmhouse kitchen,
There is a big copper kettle,
In the farmhouse kitchen,
The water pump stands tall,
In the farmhouse kitchen,
The shelves are filled with interesting foods.

In the farmhouse kitchen,
The oil lamps are bright and warm,
In the farmhouse kitchen,
There are old, heavy scales,
In the farmhouse kitchen,
The tempting smell of pancakes
Is wafting through the air.

Chris Polley (11)
Woodland View Middle School

A Personification Poem

I can cause tidal waves,
I can blow snowflakes.

I can carry house tops
And pull down trees.

I am invisible,
But what I do, all can see.

I can be as angry as a bull,
Or as gentle as a rabbit.

Sally Mellows (10)
Woodland View Middle School

A Personification Poem

I like being tall, above everything else.
Feeling the breeze brushing through my leaves.

I like it when it rains because it feeds me water
I don't get cold because my leaves keep me warmer.

Providing shelter, I am helpful,
At Christmstime I look beautiful.

I nearly fall over in the wind
But instead I twist and bend.

Chelsie Riley (10)
Woodland View Middle School

HAPPINESS

Happiness is yellow.
It smells like spaghetti bolognaise.
It tastes like an apple.
It sounds like wind blowing.
It feels like a pillow.
It lives on a mountain.

Christopher Ellis (10)
Woodland View Middle School

LIFE IN SPACE

Life in space, it's a wonderful place,
Sun is hot and round,
Mars is red,
I feel weightless inside the rocket,
I am floating around!
I have to sort of swim around to eat and drink,
I sleep floating around
And wake up at the top of the rocket!

Alannah Hogarth (8)
Woodland View Middle School

WINTER POEM

I saw frost going around and my fingers go all numb.
As I walk in the freezing snow
Children are building snowmen.
As I go by where people go past
I hear echoes coming
Is what I hear
Children going on sledges is what I see.
Puddles are frozen as ice,
Things sparkle nice and bright.
That makes me feel like it's Christmas Day
I love Christmas.

Christopher Betts (8)
Woodland View Middle School

Orbiting In Space

I love space.
It is a very big place!
It is very, very cold, flying in space.
I'm so happy to be in a lovely big space shuttle.
I love it up here.
There's nothing to fear and it's always lasting here.
It never is hot, it never is warm.
It is freezing cold!
I never will come down
And never will see my fantastic big home.

Lauren Carey (8)
Woodland View Middle School

HAPPINESS

Happiness is light blue.
It smells like vanilla ice cream.
Happiness tastes like Coke.
It sounds like a bird flying in the air.
It feels like silk.
Happiness lives in the sky.

Jordan Bezants (10)
Woodland View Middle School

PEACE

Peace is white,
It smells sweet,
Peace tastes like sugar,
It sounds like the beautiful song of a bird,
It feels like soft white feathers,
Peace lives in a dove.

Georgia Livock (9)
Woodland View Middle School

DEATH

Death is *black*
It smells like rotten apples
Death tastes like gone off bitter
It sounds like wolves howling
It feels like lightning
Death lives in the valley from the shadow of death.

Karl England (10)
Woodland View Middle School

HOPE

Hope is pale blue,
It smells like rose petals,
Hope tastes like vanilla ice cream,
It sounds like sweet music playing softly,
It feels like a silk cloth.
Hope lives in the fluffy clouds of Heaven.

Rosanna Wise (9)
Woodland View Middle School

Happiness

Happiness is blue,
It smells like curry.
Happiness tastes like coconut ice cream,
It sounds like snowball fighting,
It feels like playing games.
Happiness lives in our hearts.

Bradley Mason (9)
Woodland View Middle School

A Personification Poem

I can flash, I can crash whilst lighting up the sky.
I come out at night when I'm infuriated.

I can change my shape into fork or dagger.
I watch over people then I flash my dagger.

I can fly out before you can see me.
I come out to play whilst frightening my prey.

I can crash into houses, I can flash over towns.
I can flash but calm in the dead of the night.

Tom Macdonald (11)
Woodland View Middle School

ORBITING IN SPACE

Astronauts go into big, big, huge space.
In a huge, big, big, huge rocket.
The stars twinkle in the moonlight that shines so well.
In the sun we see the one we know well.
The aliens they fly to old and new planets.
In their spaceships to Space Zany.
The world we can see is as small as a blueberry.

Serena Barnes (8)
Woodland View Middle School

The Dumb Baby

The baby wriggled and wriggled, it didn't stop!
I wasn't pleased with the way it pulled my hair!
It had my sweets.
It sucked its dummy
The baby cried all the time!
It was so cute.

David Hadley (8)
Woodland View Middle School

WINTER POEM

It was snowing
The snow was very soft and wet.
It was chilly,
Frozen, snowy, freezing, cold, crispy, blizzard.
The snow is falling,
People are building snowman.
People have Christmas dinner and Christmas trees,
Foxes are creeping about.
My hands are very cold and dripping with icicles,
The decorations of a Christmas are making my eyes glow.
Children be quiet
Ssh, ssh!
Everything is pretty at Christmastime.
The snow is very cold.
It makes me shiver like I need to wear socks!

Lewis Attwood (9)
Woodland View Middle School

ORBITING IN SPACE

The spacecraft is ready to take off . . .
3 . . . 2 . . . 1 . . . go!
The ship blasts off
Leaving the last astronaut behind
With the scientist.
We got into space
Safe and sound.

Our food is flying in the air
Wrapped in foil and plastic!
The space station is connecting
One piece at a time!

Ben Porter (8)
Woodland View Middle School

Orbiting In Space

I am in space and everything is silent.
I can see lots of planets out of the window of the rocket.
I haven't seen anything so magical in all my life.
There are shooting stars
And the moon
Everything is wonderful.
I am feeling soft and amazed at the same time.
I don't know what to do.
The thing I love most,
Catching things that float around,
That was my favourite thing!

Marie Goffin (8)
Woodland View Middle School

AUTUMN DAYS

A utumn days are getting colder.
U nder leaves there are caterpillars munching away.
T rees are getting barely any leaves.
U nderground there are animals getting ready to hibernate.
M any birds are migrating to leave.
N ow grass is getting dew.

D ays go by soon, ice could be on your wall,
A nd autumn is here.
Y ou could freeze in bed and catch a cold.
S quirrels are looking for their nuts.

Liam Barnett (8)
Woodland View Middle School

A Personification Poem

When the sun is setting, just about to fall,
I drape my dark cloak over all.

You go to bed, I cast my spell,
Go and dream your dreams and dream them well.

My spell is over, I hear a call,
It says, 'Your hours are done, so let your black cloak fall.'

The sun comes back, as everyone can see,
I go to bed because it's too light for me!

Sam Davison (10)
Woodland View Middle School

SPACE

Space is limitless,
Space is mysterious,
It's the giant of the universe,
It's forever unending.

Space is infinitive,
Space is unknown,
It's engulfed by darkness,
It's unimagined.

Space is black,
Space is colossal,
It's like a sheet of blackness,
It's an immense black hole.

Space is dark and maybe dangerous,
Space has asteroids and meteorites flying around,
It's like a constant night,
It is the sight of space!

Paul Barker (12)
Woodland View Middle School

WINTER POEM

The season of winter has arrived.
My face, feet and hands are feeling like blocks of ice.

I see children building snowmen in their gardens.
Christmas lights are sparkling in windows.

I hear the roar of fun and laughter
Of people sledging down the hillside.
The howling wind is echoing in my ears.
Icicles are glistening in the hazy sunshine.

I just feel I want to sit by a blazing fire
And curl up into a ball and get to sleep.
Snowflakes are falling onto my hand.
Dads are doing what they do the most.
Children are playing with their brothers or sisters in the snow.
In the end we have lots of fun.
I'm having fun with my mum.

Lauren Hyde (8)
Woodland View Middle School

Winter Poem

I saw the snowflakes falling from the sky.
I sat by my window to see all the bare trees.
The icicles on the top of my house glowing from the whiteness.
I made a white snowman.
It felt frozen when I touched it.
The sledge I had out, ran down to the bottom of my garden.
I saw Christmas lights everywhere.
I wish I was there.
The robin ate all the food on the bird table.
I saw a hedgehog hibernating in the garden.
I put some food out for him.
There were boys and girls having a snowball fight.
It looked exciting.
I saw a frozen pond next to my house.
It was very quiet and calm.
In the road I made an angel that my brother destroyed.
Then I heard the roaring in the wind.

Amy Patterson (8)
Woodland View Middle School

The Legacy

The black hole engulfed by darkness,
The unimagined, mysterious universe,
The limitless zone of nothingness,
Death waiting for a glimpse of light,
The giant of the blackness,
Swallowing up life itself.
A human nightmare.

The next stage for the human race,
Homes for the homeless,
Waiting to be explored.
A cosmatic universe with everything,
The new age,
The scientific cosmos,
A never dying ghost.

Matthew Plane (11)
Woodland View Middle School

NEPTUNE

Cold as ice in a frozen river,
Lethal to the breath,
It'll find you, catch you, eat up,
And take you away with violent winds.

You'll be hurled up like a microscopic bug,
Never to be seen again.
No signs of life will you find here,
Because nothing can ever survive.

When you're here you haven't a chance,
Nothing can save you from the methane gas.
You'll never leave this ghastly planet,
The forbidding planet of Neptune.

Hazel Pointer (11)
Woodland View Middle School

WINTER POEM

When the snow falls
My fingers start to glow,
The sounds of leaves crunching
And the wind is howling.

Icicles dangling
Frozen puddles,
Robins tweeting, looking for food
Building snowmen.

My fingers are numb
And my cheeks are pinched,
Blizzards are blowing
People riding on skates.

My voice echoes
I can see a Christmas tree,
Just the one for me
People having snowball fights!

Snowflakes falling
Snow drifting down from the sky,
Water dripping from an icicle
When it snows, I get a tingling feeling.

Luke Roper (9)
Woodland View Middle School

AUTUMN

A utumn is the time of year when animals hibernate.
U mbrellas are up again because rain's coming.
T rees are getting bare because leaves are falling.
U nder the ground badgers hibernate.
M ulticolours from the leaves spread.
N uts have gone to squirrels.

D ays are getting shorter, nights are getting longer.
A ssembly has gone harvesty.
Y esterday was sunny, today is gloomy.
S unny days are over for the year.

Lily Mackie (8)
Woodland View Middle School

Going To Space

When the booster warmed up, the rocket shot in the air.
I was tumbling and stumbling all around, until I started floating
in the air.
When I opened my sandwich, it just started to float,
I just couldn't catch it!
Everyone stumbled to get it.
At last we got it!
But it wasn't the end.
Juice cartons everywhere and everyone's food was flying around!
Four days later we landed with a *bump!*
Which made everyone *jump!*
We all put our spacesuits on.
I pushed a button and the door shot open.
We were shocked!
We thought we were dreaming, we tried to open our eyes,
We were still there!
We walked on the crusty ground.
It was brilliant!

Chloe McEwen (8)
Woodland View Middle School

WINTER POEM

Everything lies glistening under a blanket of snow,
Frost comes to tell the world, so everything may know
The secret of winter falling upon the world below.

As snowflakes pick their way across the sky
And tired robins heavily sigh
And now all the world will know why and how,
Winter unfolds and how people catch colds
And how much nature holds.

John Mellows (9)
Woodland View Middle School

A Victorian Farmhouse Kitchen

It's dark outside in the rain,
As I stand in the cosy, warm kitchen looking through
the windowpane,
Bright flames flicker in the black stove,
Making shadows on the wall move,
As peaceful thoughts run through my brain.

The oil lamp stands on the table giving a yellow light,
Making objects look very bright.
Steam is coming from the copper kettle
And the scales in the corner are made of shiny metal.
Everything is warm and comforting on a cold winter's night.

My feet feel cold on the hard flagstone floor,
As I reach out for the pantry door.
The pump is dripping water in the white sink,
I hold my cup underneath to get a refreshing drink.
I feel happy and content though the rain does pour.

Alex Castle (10)
Woodland View Middle School

Winter

Winter is here, a layer of sparkling snow.
The trees are bare with crispy leaves on the chilly ground.
Underneath the frosty ground the animals sleep.
The skinny flowers lay underneath the ground.
The brightness has disappeared.
The air is freezing, like the North Pole.
The cold is about to come here.
Leaves all rough and crispy.
It is fun to go sledding and skiing.
There is frost, snow turns to ice.
My toes go numb.
All of the ponds start to freeze.
It is fun to play snowballs.
Winter is a calm time.
The snow looks like a white cinema screen.

Jordan Hunt (8)
Woodland View Middle School

A Dolphin

A dolphin that dives in the water,
It swishes his tail like a whale.
A dolphin glides through the air,
Like a bird.
A dolphin is an excellent swimmer.
A dolphin is silky,
Like a wet piece of seaweed.
A dolphin's skin is pale blue,
Like the sky.
Flippers splash in the water
When a dolphin is about.

Alex Nicholls (8)
Woodland View Middle School

THE ROBIN

The robin jumps from tree to tree,
Showing off her big red breast,
Making a nest,
Before having a rest.
With her little thin legs,
She lays some eggs.
With her huge, bold eyes,
Flying around looking for food,
She gets in a mood
Because she can't find food.
Her silky brown coat
To keep her warm.
Finds some berries on a bush
And rushes home
To her chicks,
Safe and sound.
A day's work is done and finished with
And she cuddles up with her chicks.

Daniel Chambers (8)
Woodland View Middle School

WINTER POEM

I walk along the path, the trees are bare.
I walk in the leaves and they make a *crunch! crunch! crunch!* sound.
My fingers have gone very numb and they feel like they are glowing.
My face is cold, soft and tingling, like snowflakes falling on my face.
The houses are covered with tinkling, white snow, like rain, but white.
My feet feel like they are shivering, like the trees do when it is windy.
The snow is falling down, like raindrops from the sky.
The wind blows, like the trees.
When winter has ended, we say goodbye.

Alice Bowen (9)
Woodland View Middle School

Tin Can Man

The tin can man
Lives in a tin can yard.

Inside an enormous bin
He wobbles just like a plate of jelly.

He has a twinkle in his eyes
And a glow to his torso.

His arms and legs are tin cans
The tins rattle and battle together.

As he scurries through the tin can yard
His head shines as the sun beams down.

He goes back to his tin can dustbin
He's had a wonderful day.

Bethany Wade (9)
Woodland View Middle School

BONFIRE NIGHT

It's Bonfire Night
As we light the rockets and dragons.
We have sparklers,
That light up the night.
We write our names in the air,
It's a wonderful sight.
We have Catherine wheels,
They spit sparks.
We light a bonfire,
It crackles away.
We throw wood on the bonfire,
The flames get higher,
As we walk home.

Isaac Barnett (8)
Woodland View Middle School

THE ROBIN

Looks down from the treetops,
Onto everything around.
As he hops through the air,
He falls to the ground.
As he scurries to the berry bush
And pinches some berries and acorns
And hurries home
And shares it with his family.

Ike Neave (9)
Woodland View Middle School

Orbiting In Space

The rocket zooms up in the clouds,
Oh the sound is loud!
Floating high up in space,
This is the coolest place!

The stars are twinkling in the sky,
With no gravity I can fly!
The sky is sparkling blue,
I hope I don't fall, *phew!*

On the space station it is fun,
I am trying to catch a floating bun!
Space is the best place to be,
Maybe someday, you'll take a trip with me!

Laura Dodds (8)
Woodland View Middle School

Spring

Spring's here
Animals have come out from their sleep
Flowers blossoming, all bright and colourful
Chicks have hatched, lambs in the field
Jumping, trying to fly
Bunnies as soft as cotton wool
Sun comes out
So children can play
But when spring's over
Summer's next
You will have to wait until next year
For more fun.

Naomi Long (9)
Woodland View Middle School

THE WINTER

Playing outside
Blankets of snow falling like cushions
Ready to play
The whole world turning white
Children playing
Roads becoming slushy
Time to put bobble hats on
Shaking trees
Snow drifting from twigs
The white glistening snow
Groups of snowmen chatting
Snowballs being hurled through the air
Tree trunks made invisible by snow.

Sam Doggett (10)
Woodland View Middle School

ANIMALS

My mum won't let me keep a rabbit
She won't let me keep a slithery snake
My mum won't let me keep a warthog
Then what will she let me keep?

My mum won't let me keep a hairy lion
She won't let me keep an octopus
My mum won't let me keep a fish
Then what will she let me keep?

My mum won't let me keep a slimy frog
She won't let me keep a cute dog
My mum won't let me keep a fluffy cat
Then what will she let me keep?

My mum won't let me keep a mouse
She won't let me keep a kangaroo
My mum won't let me keep a bear
Then what will she let me keep?

So under my bed I keep a pet ant
And up in the attic I keep a
Secret rat!

Jordan Paul Reed (9)
Woodland View Middle School

There Was An Old Teacher From School

There was an old teacher from school,
Who died and turned into a ghoul.
He scared all the kids
And all the old bids,
Dead was the old teacher from school.

Tom Joy (10)
Woodland View Middle School

AUTUMN

Autumn is the time of year when the floor is covered with
golden leaves,
Autumn is the time of year when the grass is jewelled,
Autumn is the time of year when leaves fall majestically off
their parent plants,
Autumn is the time of year when animals are storing food
and getting prepared for winter,
Autumn, autumn.

Autumn is the time of year when the days are getting shorter,
Autumn is the time of year when people start to wrap up warm,
Autumn is the time of year when fungi erupts from the ground,
Autumn is the time of year when churches are full of food
for Harvest Festival,
Autumn, autumn.

Neil Robert Hardman (9)
Woodland View Middle School

Deep Blue

In the deep blue
With mythical creatures swimming around
Mermaids dance while fairies sing
The sea's music box
And up above the fairies can hear
The golden light fairies are brushing
Their shimmering hair.
In the dark, deep blue.

Eloise Fitt (9)
Woodland View Middle School

Dreaming Dreams

I dreamed that I could fly,
Fly up to the sky,
Above the clouds,
Higher than the birds.
I dreamed that I had wishes,
Neverending wishes,
I wished that I had ice cream,
Chocolate here and there and everywhere.
I dreamed that I was in space,
Floating around in the stratosphere,
Walking on the moon,
Looking down at Earth.
I dreamed I was in the snow,
Throwing snowballs at my friends,
Making a snowman which comes to life.
But they were just dreams . . .
'Max, Max!' yelled my teacher,
'How many times do you daydream in class?'

Conor Lake (10)
Woodland View Middle School

TREASURE

Searching for treasure
Deep in the ocean bed
Exploring a wet, old, rotting ship
Ghosts of the past.

Hunting in and around the shipwreck
Finding bones and skulls
Pirates at a long table
Sitting on their chairs.

On the table lays the treasure
In a massive golden bowl
Ramming coins in our pockets
And swimming back to shore.

Daniel Bland (10)
Woodland View Middle School

TIGER

I pad softly around,
Do they really care?
I wonder, just wonder
If anyone's really there.

The bars of my cage taunt me,
As I sit and softly cry.
Memories float through my brain,
I just think, *why, oh why.*

With my stripes, black as coal,
My orange fur like the sun,
All I can remember,
Are the days when I had fun.

I feel so angry,
I know that they don't care,
I look so sad and dirty,
Like someone who takes no care.

This food tastes like grit,
I can't swallow it for tears,
All those people think I'm dangerous,
Don't come near because of fear.

Is this the end for me?
They want to take me away,
Because I know not where I'm going,
There's no more left to say.

Charlotte Leeming (12)
Woodland View Middle School

Sadness

Sadness is the plague we all fear,
It grabs hold of you and pulls you down,
It crawls in the murkiest corners of the Earth,
Living on tears.
We feel it, we smell it and we sense it,
But we do not see it.
It's just a few wisps of black smoke,
Penetrating the Earth.
It washes over you like a bucket of ice-cold water,
Sending a shiver up your spine,
It breaks you down like a sledgehammer,
Until you're gone.
But then there's hope,
You see the sun,
The corners of your mouth lift
And you break into the sunlight.

Jenny Crothers (11)
Woodland View Middle School

There Was A Young Lady From York

There was a young lady from York
She swallowed a big, golden cork
It got stuck in her throat
Then she gave a big croak
That silly young lady from York.

Rachael Sarsby (11)
Woodland View Middle School

The Second World War

The roar of gunshot,
The stench of blood,
While all the dead bodies lay there and rot.

The red devil of blood,
Stain their families' lives,
While their loved ones lay there in the mud.

The screaming of the dying,
Like a droning siren
And family and friends sit there crying.

The war was awful
And many people died,
The results of war were awful.

Edward Allison (11)
Woodland View Middle School

Morning Rays

The sun is like the morning rays
Shining like a mystery daze
The sun is like a mystery star
Shining wherever you are
The sun is like a mystery star.

Do you ever wonder how it got there?
Do you ever stop and stare?
Floating up in the air
Shining for all of us to share
But some people just don't care
The sun is always there.

Charlotte Morgan (12)
Woodland View Middle School

There Was An Old Man From Norwich

There was an old man from Norwich
Who got stuck in a bowl of porridge
He finally got out
And started to shout
He was the most annoyed man in Norwich.

Reece Smith (10)
Woodland View Middle School

MENORCA

The sun winks with glowing rays,
The golden sand on the bays.
Rocks on the shore, like big, huge claws,
Sea like blue glistening gems.

The food I eat is a treat.
Villa like a mansion.
You can't even imagine!
The pool has little wrinkles rippling across the surface.

My mum says, 'Let's go!'
I shout, *'No!'*
On the plane I go to sleep,
I don't even make a peep.

Phillip Fordham (12)
Woodland View Middle School

A Snake Kenning

A colourful carnivore
A slithering slur
A poisonous stick
A scaly skin
A hissing thing.

Benjamin Moon (11)
Woodland View Middle School

TREASURE

Searching for treasure,
Thousands of miles down in the Atlantic ocean.

Discovering abandoned ships
Sea creatures of the past
Diving deep in scuba divers' suits
Sharks following
Wondering what will happen
Piranhas - shadows in the ocean
Monsters coming after them.

Danny Wigger (9)
Woodland View Middle School

THE BLACK STALLION OF CHESTER

Searching for his rider
On a dark, moonlit night
Moonlight shining on his glossy coat
Galloping down the cobbled streets
In the silent night
His echoing hooves clattering through the deserted streets
And his velvet-soft nose
The ruffles in his coat, like ice cream
Despairing, he lowers his head
Then a shock of joy
As he finds his rider.

Shona Hannant (10)
Woodland View Middle School

SHIPWRECK

Swimming in the sea one day,
I came upon a shipwreck,
It was called the Mary Rose
And it was rotting through.

As I was seeking for treasure,
I came upon a key,
Then I found a wooden chest
And shouted out with glee.

I pulled open the lid
And as soon as I did,
I was engulfed in the gleaming glory
Of *gold.*

Jordan Peter Hill (10)
Woodland View Middle School

THE LEOPARD

A leopard zooms through the air,
Showing off his big, black spots,
As he passes a big, brown bear,
Who gives him a scary glare,
Yellow fur and lots of it,
Flying in the misty air.

He jumps for his prey,
He's been trying to catch a mouse all day,
He zooms through the scorching desert
Without a care.
The other animals stop to look and stare.
He goes back home to eat a bone.
The day is over.

Charlotte Stephens (9)
Woodland View Middle School

AUTUMN DAYS

A corns and conkers start to fall, so we can get them
U p in the trees the leaves fall down
T rees are preparing for the winter
U pon the ground there are lots of leaves
M any leaves are now red, yellow and brown
N oises of birds, you can hear.

D ays get shorter
A nimals get food, ready to hibernate
Y our hands and nose go white
S piky cones of conkers.

Amy Urry (9)
Woodland View Middle School

TIN CAN MAN

The tin can man
Lives in a tin can yard
He drinks oil to stop himself rusting
He is enormous and magnificent
He wobbles like a piece of jelly
He has a twinkle in his eyes
And a glow in his torso
His arms and legs are tin cans
His torso is a dustbin
He is a metallic silver
He gives you a glare
But then he scuffs his feet
Clickety, clang, clatter.

Alexandra Slaughter (8)
Woodland View Middle School

WINTER

Snow is covering everything, like a carpet.
Slippery ice to run and skid on.
Bare trees shivering in the freezing cold air.
Everything looks like one big, white screen.
Get wrapped up warm.
Scarves, gloves and a woolly hat.
The snow is sparkling
Like crystals on the ground.
Everyone running and throwing snowballs.
There's people on sledges having fun.
Kids are building snowmen with carrots and stones.
Snowflakes falling into your hair.
There's snow here, there's snow there,
There's snow everywhere.
The ice is all hard and rocky.
The snow is soft, smooth and freezing cold.

Charlotte Curson (8)
Woodland View Middle School

WINTER

Not long ago
Snow appeared from the distance,
Sparkling snow glistened as it fell,
People sledding on the ice,
People playing snowball fights,
People picking off icicles,
Sparkling crystals glistened from the ground.
Shiny diamonds on the ground,
People dressed warm,
Sparkly snow lead the way.
Woolly hats, fluffy scarves.
Some people building snowmen.
Green grass hidden under the snow,
Freezing temperatures appear from nowhere.

Thomas Freeman (8)
Woodland View Middle School

WINTER

A giant carpet of snow covers everything.
Footsteps uncover a tiny bit of summer.
The water is now ice.
Whistling wind zooms past me.
Snowflakes falling fast.
Trees are as bare as skeletons.
The air is like the air from an air conditioner.
Snowmen on patrol.
Hedgehogs are nowhere to be seen.
The cold is unbearable.
Slippery, slidy ice.
Wrap up warm.
Everything's white.
Let's sledge.
I'm cold.
Snow has taken over.
Icicles hang down.
Snow-coated branches.
Cold, bitter wind.
Drive carefully,
Beware of the ice.
The gritters are out, gritting.

Shaun Earl (8)
Woodland View Middle School